Peter Coates is a retired doctor. He trained in Haematology at University College Hospital in London between 1981 and 1988. Between 1988 and 2015 he was part of the team that built up the Clinical Haematology services at The Queen Elizabeth Hospital, King's Lynn. Since retirement, he has undertaken voluntary work with Churches Together in King's Lynn, Macmillan Cancer Support, local hospital and prison chaplaincies, and is currently a trustee of the Norfolk Hospice Tapping House and the King's Lynn Night Shelter for the homeless. He is a member of a local poetry group called Centre Poets.

A New Bottom Line

This book of poetry is dedicated to the New Bottom Line which is proposed by Rabbi Michael Lerner in his book *Revolutionary Love: A Political Manifesto to Heal and Transform the World*. Rabbi Michael and his American group 'The Network of Spiritual Progressives' (info@spiritualprogressives.org) propose introducing a new bottom line by regular peer review of companies and institutions. This new bottom line is as follows:

'We propose to judge our institutions, our economy, our political lives, our legal system, our cultural institutions, our educational system, and every aspect of our society as productive, efficient, or rational to the extent that they maximise our human capacities to be loving, generous, and caring towards each other and towards the Earth, ethically and environmentally responsible, and committed to social, economic, and environmental justice; and the extent to which they promote joy, playfulness, compassion and empathy, self-acceptance, humour, and aesthetic creativity, health and thanksgiving for life in all its forms, love of learning, science and literature, repentance and forgiveness, treatment of all human beings as embodiments of the sacred and not just instrumentally as a means to our own ends, and a response to the universe and our planet Earth that is filled with awe, wonder and radical amazement (rather than seeing them as resources to fill human needs).'

Peter Coates

GENERATION CARE

Poetry for a Caring Society

AUSTIN MACAULEY PUBLISHERS™

LONDON * CAMBRIDGE * NEW YORK * SHARJAH

A CIP catalogue record for this title is available from the British Library.

ISBN 9781398454651 (Paperback)
ISBN 9781398454668 (Hardback)
ISBN 9781398454675 (ePub e-book)

www.austinmacauley.com

First Published 2022
Austin Macauley Publishers Ltd®
1 Canada Square
Canary Wharf
London
E14 5AA

My thanks go to Jesus for a peaceful life, to Jane for sharing my life, to Paul Berry and the members of Centre Poets for sharing their poetry lives, and to Paul Berry and to Anne Raumann for proofreading and their expert knowledge of punctuation. My thanks to Rabbi Michael Lerner and Cat Zavis for their inspirational view of a more caring and empathic society. My writing has been influenced by many books but I would particularly like to mention the work of Anne Case and Angus Deaton which is recorded in their book *Deaths of Despair* and the *Future of Capitalism*.

Table of Contents

1. Come Close

Come close, my love,
Come closer still,
That I may hear you breathe,
That I may rest my head on you,
And you will never leave.
Come close.

Come close, my friend,
Come closer still,
That we may intertwine
Our worldly vulnerabilities,
Our deepest strengths align.
Come close.

Come close, my joy,
Come closer still,
And talk to me your way,
That I may listen to your voice
For ever and a day.
Come close.

We're buying a priceless jewel;
We're escaping the icy cruel;
We're skilled with a perfect tool;
We're energy launching renewal.

Come close, my love,
Come closer still,
That I may hug you tight
To thank you for your loyalty,
And caring ever bright.
Come close.

Stay close, my love,
Stay closer still,
As love swirls round us both:
Recognised, confirmed and rare,
Progenitor of growth.
Stay close.

18/12/20

2. No Judgement Garden

Love, what do you say to us,
We who can't agree?
We'll build 'No Judgement Garden',
That's how it will be.

We'll build 'No Judgement Garden',
No money is involved,
It's just what people want to do,
It's nothing being sold.

We can judge the outcomes,
To know what really works;
But after judging people,
Then, deep rejection lurks.

Some wouldn't want to enter,
A choice that seems quite mad,
Perhaps they cannot see the peace;
The calm they never had.

We'll walk the open-minded path,
We'll speak about the pain,
And those who wrongly blamed themselves,
Can find their path again.

We'll view 'No Judgement Garden',
The sun is warm and bright,
Curious to know our dreams;

Escaping from the night.

By the 'Unbiased River',
You'll whisper how you feel,
Impartial and unprejudiced,
Revealing needs are real.

We'll speak about disinterest,
We're balanced and detached,
So then we'll find our values,
With understanding hatched.

Past the 'Mountains of Dispassion',
And by 'Objective's Lake',
Our dream to value people,
And not to money make.

Through the 'Wood of Charity',
Or seated for the view,
The flowers of forgiveness,
Will fill the scene anew.

By the 'Enlightened Vineyard',
A table will be set,
And we will eat benevolence;
Just happy that we met.

The wine, we'll call it 'Tolerance'
Uncritical the chat;
Acceptance is the second course,
And freedom after that.

Our listening observant,
Our minds will understand,
Although we really can't agree,
But I can shake your hand.

The crowds are at one table,
Of sacrifice and love;
They'll make their own decisions,
While guided from above.

09/03/2021

3. A Vast Existence

Give me a view of the Norfolk sky,
That lovely blue,
Where shapes of cotton wool drift by;
A vast existence.

Give me a view of the Norfolk sky,
In an age of dysfunctional thought,
Where clouds make shapes like animal faces,
Changing, drifting, merging, lifting;
A vast existence.

Give me a view of the Norfolk sky,
When I am stressed or hurt,
Where sunny clouds will shine like pearls,
And rays beam down through cloudy curls;
A vast existence.

Millennia past evolved our minds,
Viewing the heavens high;
Perhaps it's why I feel depressed,
When buildings hide the sky.

Give me a view of the clear night sky,
That Norfolk sky,
That vast existence,
Where countless stars vault rustling trees,
Or the yellow moon shimmers on rippling seas,
A silent sky;

An awesome sky;
A vast existence.

Give me a view of the Norfolk sky,
That high sky,
That vast existence.
No me, no lack,
No world, no work,
And no distress;
Just joy;
A sense of God;
A vast existence.

There is no judgment given;
There are no violent acts
In looking up at beauty,
From the grief of imprisoning facts.

For God is the only
Valid vast existence.

27/09/2017

4. Moments of Joy

Are you tired, grumpy or shy
From the long journey?
Clinging to your mum,
Eyes averted.

But soon we'll be chasing,
Playing hide and seek,
Or exploring,
Finding what we're not supposed.

I'll be a monster
Clump, clump clumping up the stairs.
You'll scream and run,
Or giggle from your hiding place;

Or we'll make a house for you,
Cushions on the sofa.
I'll peer in at the window;
The big bad wolf.

You'll find a long cardboard tube.
When its end's behind my ear,
You'll shout,
I'll jump.

We can dance to the music,
I'll make a treasure hunt for you,
And fill the paddling pool with water,

Or we'll go to the beach to play.

I hope you never grow up completely;
I haven't.

30/06/2019

5. Our Spirit Minds

Disturbing; you're unhappy,
Anybody, anywhere.
Can't we all be family,
Conversing while we care?

Families can fracture,
Breaking fragile ties.
Desiring leads to torture,
And then there's no replies.

I live alone; I'm feeling ill;
I'm frightened I might die.
I'm thinking the computer
Might help me with AI.
I turn it on; I fire it up,
I'm giving it a try.
Because it says my password's wrong,
It gives me no reply.

(Is there anyone I can discuss this with? Please!)

Engage, converse and listen,
Solving problems any size.
Anger breaks the magic spell,
And leads to no replies.

Complex, failed, diverse or odd,
Together reaching highs,

'til war blocks conversations,
Extinguishing replies.

And when a group engage in prayer,
Mob tyranny defied,
The conversations full of life,
And peace is the reply.

The landscape can be massive,
It's peaceful and it's still.
Can you see our spirit minds,
The universe will fill?

27/06/2020

6. Exodus

No God, you say,
Just death's disaster.
But if he gave us bread and wine,
Standing on the Karman Line,
Would you believe
Our master?

No God, you say,
Just death's disaster.
Look down at curving white and blue,
With hosts of travellers, me and you.
Would you believe
Our master?

No God, you say,
Just death's disaster.
But if the dead should join the host,
Fleeing sin from coast to coast,
Would you believe
Our master?

Father, forbid
That pain and bereavement should drag us down,
Away from your infinite gift,
Away from the joy we have within;
Your joy, that is our lift.

No God, you say,
Just death's disaster.
But if we joined our minds to pray,
One mind we'd be upon that day.
Would you believe
Our master?

No God, you say,
Just death's disaster.
But would you follow light years far,
To new homes near that distant star,
And never leave,
Our master?

08/09/17

7. I Can't Touch
Your Magnificence

White ghost of woodland edge,
What is your beauty?
Suddenly you appear,
A lone silent spirit in the air;
Beauty in a harsh world,
Raising my spirits.

Silent spirit,
Your wings are motionless
And yet you drift forward,
In perfect control.

Does your huge white heart-shaped face mean love?
Or is your heart cut vertically,
Like your beautiful white face,
By a predatory nose and beak?

And when your wings
Slowly caress the air,
Is it for the beauty of your spirit?
Or for the silence of the hunt?
But I can only watch,
From a distance;
I can't touch your magnificence.
You are a rare beauty.

26/02/20

8. The Essence of
God Is Mercy

When will oceans stop drowning me and space stop sucking my breath away?
When will fire stop peeling my skin and cold stop freezing my blood?
When will work stop overwhelming me and money stop giving me debt?
When will falls stop killing me and blasts stop blowing me away?
When will disasters stop engulfing me and earthquakes stop crushing me?
When will bullets stop splattering my blood and disease stop eating me from the inside?
When will power stop herding me into pens and the law stop judging me?
When will enemies disappear and consciousness expand to fill space and time?

Oh Christ, it's when we become mercy.

18/11/19

9. Deaths of Despression

Who am I?
And who are you?
And will we ever know
Why those of 50 kill themselves,
Why they're despairing so?

Why is it in America,
They're dying of despair?
Did you really love them?
Did you really care?

Who destroyed their life's chance?
To China moved their jobs?
Who destroyed community?
Happiness turned to sobs?

Did you love technology?
And spent your time on that?
Or love extracting money?
Or those exams you sat?

Your massive cost of healthcare,
And profits made from drugs.
Did you love analgesics
More than giving hugs?

Is merit really merciful?
Is merit really fair?

Is merit ever humble?
Does merit really care?

Did you think yourself important
While you didn't see their pain?
And now six hundred thousand,
You'll never see again.

Is merit individual?
Does merit ever share?
Does merit like to dominate?
Does merit really care?

So, who are you?
And who is Christ,
The church that you ignore?
If only you had gone there,
And entered in the door.

20/04/21

10. Some Stay

Some,
Crash around;
Their vast motivation bouncing,
Like ping-pong balls
In electric blenders;
Some.

Some say,
'Collision's inevitable,
Dramas and agonies unavoidable,'
Some say.

Some say sacred,
So that puerile violence
Could die,
Showing domination's a lie.
Some say sacred.

Some stay sacred,
So truth could reign,
And independence gain,
Where some stay.

Some say sacred Trinity,
Where communities share,
And sacred fragments there,
Ride and hide
In foes.

Some say.

Some stay sacred:
They get out of the boat,
And walk towards Jesus,
Who hides in their rival,
For peace and survival;
Embracing the Trinity,
Where love is infinity.
Some stay.

07/06/2020

11. Menol Elf

Mum addicted, Dad unknown,
There's more out there,
Moving out.

Can't get food, a roof,
But there's plenty of abuse,
Moving out.

I'd like to make a complex plan
The basis of my life.
My fractal brain just throws me thoughts,
Of violence with a knife.
'Menol elf'.

Universal credit's here,
All password protected;
Why it is then that mine won't work?
Complexities undetected?
Is it 'Menol elf'?

Please God, you're not a computer, are you?
So I hit it.
Police say;
'Menol elf'.

I'm still keen to move on out,
But not while I'm in prison.
There's lots of gangs and violence here

And plenty of derision.
(They all got 'Menol elf').

Best kill myself,
No hope for me, where thoughtlessness surrounds.
No conversation, no reply
No mercy can be found.

02/07/19

12. Warm Water

Can we combine with you?
Fountain of light,
River of wisdom,
Submersing flood of love.

Can we work with you?
Spring of creation,
Source of reality,
Gradient of energy.

Can we engage with you?
Depth of mercy,
Tsunami of justice,
Rapids of knowledge.

Can we experience you?
Rain of understanding,
Drink of equity,
Pool of peace.

Can we drink with you?
Ocean of oneness,
Harmony of solitude,
Hydration of life.

Can we be at peace with you?
Waterfall of faith,
Geiser of wholesomeness,

Flow of cleansing grace.

Can we depend on you?
Well of glory,
Droplets of diversity,
Trickle of friendship.

Can we know you?
Wash of hope,
Mist of mystery,
Sparkle of dignity,
Tide of truth.

Can we be your church?
Drifting in disinterest,
Silently percolated with humility,
Bathed in beatitudes.

13/04/2020

13. Not Care

If I were –
Working for money,
Not care,
Working for myself,
Not care,
Working for the corporation,
Not care,
Working for politics,
Not care,
Working for the media,
Not care,
Working to judge,
Not care,
Working to dominate,
Not care,
Working to reject,
Not care,
Working with violence,
Not care,
Working to consume,
Not care,
I'd get hell,
Not care.

How about you?

14/06/2021

14. The Infinite Joy of Repentance

What value my dreams?
In a history of dreams,
In a history of conflict,
That symptom of failed repentance,
In an ocean of dreams.

If I could dream God's dream
I would dream of repentance:
Of sin rejected,
Of naked humility,
Of Christ crucified,
Of your good dreams fulfilled,
In forgiveness and prayer.

Then my dreams are our dreams,
A shared consciousness,
An ocean of dreams,
An ocean of repentance.

Then Lord we invite you into our minds,
Where gently, repeatedly, you wash in,
As waves wash the seashore,
As reality repeatedly corrects,
Washing the spirit,
In waves of repentance.

An ocean of repentance
Becomes an ocean of faith;

An ocean of faith,
Becomes the Kingdom of God,
Just as Jesus said it would.

What value my story now?
Since I bought your eternity,
With my repentance,
And I paid with the life of Christ.

Your love became our life;
My story became our story;
My isolation became our joy;
My ignorance became our knowledge;
My grief became our success,
In the infinite joy of repentance.

15. Prescribing Gold

I'd like to be a doctor
In an office made of glass,
It's totally transparent
And not the usual farce.

I'd have a gold prescription pad
Gold standard's my command.
I'd see all those who wanted help
Perfection they'd demand.

They wouldn't need examination
History, tests, exsanguination;
Harmony with all creation
Solves their needed adaptation.

I'd prescribe them resurrection
On my golden pad:
Wholesome body, wholesome mind,
An end to going mad.

In a changed reality
Leaving all insanity,
Banishing all cruelty
For wholesomeness and harmony.

And I'd prescribe them resurrection
For their dead most dear,
The ones they thought they'd never meet

But only shed a tear.

They'd say you can't deliver this
I'm suing for a ban;
I'd say you're absolutely right
But I know a man who can.

It's Jesus.

08/12/18

16. Face Up Death

Face up, Death,
Stop hiding in the shadows.
Face up Death and tell me;
Are you really useful,
Or just a waste of tears?

For we are all witnesses;
It's everywhere we look;
Forced into our faces;
The monstrous news;
The murderous stories;
The merciless violence.

How proudly we proclaim it;
How we strut about,
Blind to our own ugliness:
Ugly monsters,
Ugly murderers,
In our ugly mercilessness.

Face up, Death.
Can you separate us?
The child pulled away again,
From the filthy motivation?

If so, Death,
Then I embrace you.

04/01/2020

17. A Visit to Brentwood Circle

I travelled here on Wednesday;
I walked through crowded scenes
And hundreds came towards me
With eyes on mobile screens.

Hundreds walked towards me
With one hand held half high
And hundreds passed unconsciously,
The screen before their eye.

Arriving here you saw me
You smiled, you knew my name;
You welcomed me like family
And let me do the same.

The joy of your existence
I felt it all the time
And also of your brothers
As I was sharing mine.

And for that time we trusted
A moment made of fun
With stories of our families
Of moments in the sun.

No thought manipulation
No power very loud
Farewells all in politeness
Then join the lonely crowd.

17/08/17

18. Silent Abundance

A hot day in May,
And peace in a prodigious landscape.
A wide path leads on,
Through spacious outstretched fields,
Of silent abundance.

The stark sun glares,
Eager to burn,
High in a clear blue sky.
But the grassy crop is young and fresh,
Slightly turquoise transparent green,
Eager to sunbathe fearlessly,
Juicy in the heat,
Of silent abundance.

The mile after mile of silent life
Shimmers warm in the distant air,
Revealing the welcome breeze,
Brushing waves of darker green,
Across the quiet abundance.

Near the path, tiny violets in the long grass,
Groups of yellow buttercups,
Shine their faces at the sun.
Tall Cow Parsley stems,
Topped by dividing stems,
Topped again by dividing stems,
Are crowned by tiny five-petalled white flowers,

Countless in their peaceful abundance.

The hawthorn hedge that lines the path
Is overhung with white blossom.
Here, a willow tree,
Like a great yacht spinnaker,
Curves its leading edge into the wind,
Its leaves individual,
Dancing in the breeze,
Sparkling in the sun,
Quietly abundant.

A frantic buzzing insect hurries by,
Buzzing louder, louder, louder – gone;
In a summer doppler flypast.
A pale blue dragonfly lands on the path,
Silent and still,
As a small white butterfly
Flutters through an oak tree's shadow.

On a hot day in May,
Walking with ease,
Facing the breeze,
Escaping all dramas,
Praising the farmers,
The growers and gardeners,
Sorrows redundance;
In silent abundance.

01/06/2020

19. Playing He or Me

On the road to Emmaus,
He says,
What are all these things?
And I say,
One question only.

Is it He or me who says,
Why do you ask?
And I say,
A game of joyous freedom.

Is it He or me says,
What is your question?
And I say,
Why do you love us?

Is it He or me says,
What is your answer?
And I say,
Am I foolish to guess,
That the answers are countless,
For those multitudes you bless?

Is it He or me says,
Tell me an answer every day.
And I say,
Yes, and can we start today?

He says,
Do you accept my Fatherhood?
And I say,
You are universal good.

Is it He or me says,
Thinking that becomes a door.
And I say,
Yes, I'll think that evermore.

Is it He or me says,
It's a game to combat sorrow.
And I say,
Can I ask again tomorrow?

01/05/2020

20. Death Starer

Wake up,
Death starer,
From power's illusions.
Don't you death stare God.

Did you aim with a cross?
Did you care or not
As a bomb exploded,
In baby's cot?
Wake up!

Did you love the power?
Did you see the hell?
Decapitating sons with your
Armour piercing shell?
Wake up!

That violent SAM
Was fired by you.
It ripped the flight,
The passengers and crew.
Wake up!

Are you haunted by the faces?
Barrel bombs falling,
In private spaces?
Wake up,
Death starer.
01/08/2019

21. Water Source

I was a drop of water,
In the ocean of mankind.
Transparent rope of gravity,
White, grey and silver lined.

I came from the water source;
Welling.

I was sparkling water,
Flowing on your head.
Falling, splashing, running
Down your face of red.

I came from the water source;
Welling up.

I was clear cool water,
Slurping on your mouth.
Blowing, burbling, bubbling,
Gravitating south.

I came from the water source;
Welling up.

My water bursting on your head,
You couldn't help but laugh,
Droplets flung through sunny rays,
I was your lifetime staff.

I came from the water source;
Emotions welling up too.

I could flow right through you,
Where enzyme action plays.
My simple humble chemistry,
Creative wholeness stays.

I came from the water source;
Welling up to eternity.

I'd be like liquid freedom,
Swirling or quite still,
I transport, mix, blend or dissolve:
A washing water mill.

I came from the water source;
Welling up to eternal life.

I come here to baptise you,
With mercy and with peace,
Jesus flowing through your life,
Your joy to never cease.

I came from the source of all;
Welling up to eternal life.

22. A Presence so Old

Have you been there,
In the presence of the big landscape,
At the creek at Burnham Overy Staithe,
When the sky overhead is blue,
Fading to near white on the horizon?

When the water is smooth and still,
Shining in the long winter sunlight;
Mirroring the motionless boat hulls and masts.

Have you been in the presence of that beautiful stillness and peace;
Have you stood beside the light, flat, smooth, perfect, glistening surface
Whose dazzling beauty demands your attention
Whose silent presence laughs at your stupid worries,
As they fly away like a flock of birds towards the sea?

Did you worry how you related?
Now, nobody cares.
We relate by being in the presence of beauty,
That's silent, still,
A teacher, a transformer, a tranquil relaxer;

Perhaps reminding each of childlike delights,
And careless days when life was playing.
How different the world seemed then?
But perhaps recaptured for this moment.
Did you feel the hushed reverence
In a presence so old?

Did you feel its nearness re-charging your existence
As if by induction?
Strengthening us in the knowledge that,
For a moment, its great presence is at peace with us.
How beautiful are you, God?
I'd like to think that we can be at peace too,
And return to childhood's carelessness, powerlessness, trust and love.

23. Our Vitriol

Pain and frustration reveal
Our vitriol.
Addicts take drugs to escape
Our vitriol.
People we judge incur
Our vitriol.
Religions fight with
Our vitriol.

Injustice?
Time to get out
Our vitriol.
Soldiers kill
With our vitriol.
Terrorists bomb
With our vitriol.
Prisoners are tortured
With our vitriol.
Landmines amputate
With our vitriol.

Demonstrators burn
With our vitriol.
When we recognised, learned;
When we accepted, learned;
That reality doesn't work;
How frequently...
It frequently doesn't work;

Our vitriol abated.

I heard of a man who was tortured to death,
He was found to have no vitriol.
Jesus, banish for ever
Our vitriol.

08/02/21

24. The War They Couldn't Stop

They've forgotten the rows and rows of dead,
And the man who shoots prisoners in the head,
Skeletal lives behind the wire,
The smell of bodies burnt by fire.
The war they couldn't stop.

They've forgotten the blood that splats with force,
They've forgotten the mud that swallows a horse,
They've forgotten the soldiers that huddle and shake,
And the best bomb ever that the scientists make.
The war they couldn't stop.

They've forgotten the illness everyone got,
The lines of deserters that had to be shot,
They've forgotten the losing of someone dear,
And the terrible feeling of living in fear.
The war they couldn't stop.

They've forgotten that spies could be anywhere,
So we have to use torture and roadblocks there,
They've forgotten the most important law:
Never, never, start a war.
A war you cannot stop.

05/02/1998

25. A Hymn to Mercy

So much violence
I would lose heart,
But every bereavement,
Magnifies the mercy
Of He who created us.

Wholly altruistic
Wholly infinite
Holy, Holy, Holy;
Mercy.

Leaving the tiring war, the instant answer;
Ignoring the desiring judgement, power's answer;
Column of justice,
Supporter of peace;
Mercy.
People binding,
People respecting,
People resurrecting;
Mercy.

Past my self-important sins;
Beyond science, maths and logic;
Or the glare of judgement;
Source of relationships,
Meaning of love,
Friend of the broken hearted;
Mercy.

Eternal transparency,
Eternal equity,
Eternal glory;
Mercy.

26. Together

Together,
Students would favour
Displaying their labour,
To learn what we know.

But workers go farther,
Their experience rather
Discovers our ignorance,
Losing their innocence.

Together,
The poor have concluded
They will be excluded.

Together,
Science would rather
Evidence gather,
Predicting behaviour
Of matter in nature.

Together,
The poor have concluded
They will be excluded.

Together,
Philosophers rather,
With unknowns, think farther,
Like the intrinsic essence

Of matter's existence,
Or that secret wondrous:
The meaning of consciousness.

Together,
The poor have concluded
They will be excluded.

In Churches Together,
The people would rather
Return to the Father
Of the Prodigal Son,
Predicting behaviour
Of Jesus, our Saviour,
Who greets the excluded,
His Kingdom concluded.

15/07/20

27. Someone Else

Can we change your reputation?
Someone else has all the wealth,
'Poor' – your current nomination,
'Charitable' better suits your health,
In love.

Can we change your reputation?
Someone else has all the work,
'Unemployed' – your current nomination,
'Honorary' better suits teamwork,
In love.

Can we change your reputation?
Someone else has all the hype,
'Ignored' – your current nomination,
'Rich' much better suits your type,
In love.

Can we change your reputation?
Someone else has family,
'Alone' – your current nomination,
'Included' suits you actually,
In love.

A new name, after blame,
A new life, after strife,
A new recognition;
Enduring cognition,

Through evolutions,
Executions,
Revolutions,
And destitutions.

Through diminutions,
Institutions,
Pollutions.
And final solutions.

Can we change your reputation?
Someone else has all the clout,
'Weak' – your current nomination,
'Serene' the life that you're about,
In love.

Can we change your reputation?
Someone else is talented,
'Failed' – your current nomination?
'Triumphant', sounding warranted,
In love.

Charitable
Honorary
Rich
Included
Serene
Triumphant.

You're a child of Christ.

25/07/20

28. Decide

What to do?
What's the worst that can happen?
Imagine it's the future;
The worst has happened,
And you're looking back.
What would you wish you had done?
Now go and do that.

16/12/20

29. Could the Whole World Fast?

Why bother to fast?
For concordance at last?
To know what it's like
To starve?
To show to mankind,
That it's very unkind,
And we know what it's like
To starve.

Yes, we know what it's like
to starve.
We're mourning vulgarity;
We're mourning barbarity.
Nine million lack parity,
With all regularity,
And starve,
(That's even with charity)
to death.
(We couldn't have more clarity).
So, they know what it's like
To starve.

So what is it like
To starve?
If food is life's attachment,
To starve is life's detachment;
And it's always weeks away
When hawsers secure,

Which hold vessels so sure,
Are cut.
A fast is formation,
It's true adaptation;
To know what it's like
To starve.

A resilience lesson:
Avoiding addiction,
Avoiding confliction,
A fast is formation,
It's true adaptation,
To know what it's like
To starve.

Why bother to fast?
Is it healing at last?
Diabetes and healing,
Now that sounds appealing,
To know what it's like
To starve.

Blood pressure's
Down;
Heart attacks
Down;
Stokes and inflammatory insults
Are down.
See immune cell generation;
DNA repair inflation.
A fast is healthy reformation,
To know what it's like
To starve.

There is brain regeneration,
Promoting nerve proliferation,

Boosting memory recollection,
And learning adaptation,
Then there is mood elevation,
Reducing chances of addiction.
It is healthy reformation,
To know what it's like
To starve.

But, but, but…
Why bother to fast?
For you never will last!
For surely, it's a pain?
A craving pain;
A cranial pain;
A weakness pain?
But why complain?
Your body adapts,
After 3 weeks elapse,
Of a regular fasting campaign.
It is healthy reformation,
To know what it's like
To starve.

We might be amazed,
The world number we raised,
Of all those who praised,
Who'd join in a fast;
The numbers are vast,
If we only asked,
Who knows what it's like
To starve?

The 1.9 billion
Who are food insecure
We fast to assure
We fast to procure

The love that's obscure,
But will always endure,
When we open the door,
To our Saviour.
He knows what it's like,
To starve.

13/02/21

30. C-C-C

'Your type hurt me,'
He said.
'Your type hurt ME,'
She said.
'Can't you see, see, see
You're alien to me?'

'Black feminist,'
He said.
'White privileged,'
She said.
'All at sea, sea, sea.
You're alien to me.'

'Don't want your figures,'
He said.
'Don't want your facts.'
She said.
'It's me, me, me,
Your alien to me.'

Lonely War.

Engulfing fear;
Dark violence;
Death.

Sweating;
Paralysing;
Syncopal;
Death.

Crushing;
Hopeless;
Impossible;
Death.

Arresting;
Chaotic;
Despairing;
Death.

But,
Momentum drives on,
And up, to healing.
Gentleness becomes us,
Imagine that:
A gentle world,
With gentle work,
Gently friendly,
Seductively happy,
In the light touch of praise.

'C-C-C,'
They said,
'See, see, see.'
'See what you convey.'
'Convey compassion,
Convey care,'
'**Convey-Compassionate-Care.**'

Empathy is,
C-C-C.

Come to tea, tea, tea.
Apple tart?
Praising each, agree,
Then giggle,
Tee-He.

09/12/2020

31. To Feel Accepted

So, what was pain invented for?

Motivation? Domination?
Or scientific gain?
Times of damage limitation?
Or times of spiritual claim?

Life is lonely,
No acceptance.

Through centuries of fighting,
For ever and a day,
Violently to dominate,
Please just go away.

Terrorism,
A symptom of rejection?
No acceptance.

Scientists will all explain,
'86 billion!' they'll exclaim,
'The neurons that are in the brain.
'That's 100 trillion nerve connections,
Working hard to make selections,

'Activating every part,
Of brain and spinal cord,
Fainting, breathless, pumping heart,'

Pain's becoming lord.
Existential death is tasted,
Loss of action; piercing sword.
Powerful emotions wasted,
Problems quickly jump on board.

Life is lonely,
No acceptance.

My thoughts: Jesus didn't suffer,
Just to show that he was tougher;
But to show for centuries long,
Inflicting suffering is wrong.

No acceptance.

Those who've passed across the veil,
May tell an even stranger tale;
Dead, and then resuscitated,
Feelings that they then related,
First time ever, felt accepted.

Acceptance?

Harmony, peace, love awaited;
With a wide awareness mated,
Morbid fear of death abated;
Spirit riding high.

Acceptance?

Is this the last subconscious lead,
Saying what we really need;
Before oblivion submerges
Our created breed.

No acceptance?

Or could this be an end of dirges?
Lasting sanity emerges,
Transcended in this sacred reign,
Life no longer suffers pain.

Acceptance?

04/07/2020

32. Welcome Anger

Welcome, Anger;
My friend from the past,
The light on my dashboard,
Of automated neural connections.

Welcome, Anger;
My radar,
My boundary,
Detecting threats
To my pride.

Welcome, Anger;
My action obligation,
I see you,
Coming over the horizon.

Welcome, Anger;
As usual,
I see you brought your friends.
Welcome Fear,
Welcome Guilt,
Welcome Shame.

Welcome, friends;
Let me prepare
To entertain you,
While you're still some way off.

Thank you for visiting me,
My reliable friends.
Sit down,
And let us talk.

What can I offer you?
What actions can I take?
Correcting my work?
Improving my skills?
Researching?
Recruiting professional help?

You know, don't you,
Old friends,
That I can't control reality,
Even through co-operation?

Will you accept that
And be placated?
Are we reconciled
Until the next time
You light up my dashboard?

08/02/21

33. Pray to Belong

Each mysterious,
We meet in our sadness,
Sharing our madness.
Could we be wrong?
Or could we bel.....
Are we listening?
Or belo.....
We're not listening.
The problem's fundamental,
We're rather judgemental,
Discrimination?
So, we don't belong.

Each mysterious,
We meet in our sadness,
Sharing our madness.
Could we be strong?
Or bel.....
Are we listening?
Or belo.....
Or belon.....
No?
Perhaps it's our fate?
Or is it a trait?
The joy to dominate,
So, we don't belong.

Each mysterious,

We meet in our sadness,
Revealing our madness.
Should we pass along?
Or bel.....
Are we listening?
Or belo.....
I said belon.....
Bel.....
B.....
No?
We'd rather rush on,
Neglect?
So, we don't belong.

Each mysterious,
We've meet in our sadness,
Displaying our madness.
Will we be long?
Or bel.....
Or belo.....
Or belon.....
Bel.....
B.....
No?
We'd rather be wrong,
Deceit?
So, we don't belong.

Each mysterious,
We meet in our sadness,
Sharing our madness.
Discussing Hong Kong.
Could we bel.....
Couldn't we belo.....
No?
We're not really listening,

It's money's conditioning
Distracts you with glistening
Disagreements are bristling,
Greed?
So, we don't belong.

If history concludes,
In shared attitudes,
Summation devices,
Of our sacrifices.

If reality's revealed,
And fates have been sealed,
Perhaps it's summation,
Of all obligation.

Behaviour, extinction,
Discrimination,
Extinction.
Domination,
Extinction.

Neglect,
Extinct.
Deceit or cheat,
Extinct.
Greed,
Extinct.

When God makes extinct,
Behaviours distinct,
Revealing his likeness,
In each person's brightness.
That's a ceremony I'd like to witness,
As uncontrollable to us in our sickness,
As death.

When conflicts are gone,
Will we all join the song?
To belong;
To belong.

Will we say to belong?
Will we stay to belong?
Will we pray to belong?
Since we travelled along,
And we waited so long.
To belong,
To belong.

06/02/2021

34. Sacred Soaring

Wonderful life,
Wonderful times,
Wonderful people,
And love.
But now illness.
Death's stalking.

What did we do right?
What did we do wrong?
What did we fail at
While singing life's song?
Death's stalking.

Our epitaph:
That we were sometimes allowed
To mitigate problems,
And that's enough.

Time to stop the endless struggle;
Time to stop being a judge;
Time to meet and sense and feel;
Time to learn what's really real:
No judgement in heaven.

Time to be in a better place;
Right here,
Right now,
A place where love can't judge or reject,

Right here,
Right now,
Where I can play with you,
Our souls sacred soaring.

25/02/21

35. Generation Care

Born in 1912,
My father's role was:
National service.
His schooling was,
Guns and money.
His generation was,
Generation war.
Substantial secret suffering.
Would he like to see,
Generation care?

Born in 1887,
His father's role was:
National service.
His schooling was,
Guns and money.
His generation was,
Generation war.
Substantial secret suffering.
Would he like to see,
Generation care?

Born in 1950,
My generation was:
National Health Service,
My schooling was,
Care and money.
My generation was,

Generation money.
Substantial secret suffering.
I would like to see,
Generation care.

When will they be born,
Generation care?
Their babies learn love,
In their first formative years?
Their National Service is care;
Their schooling is care;
Their full employment is care.
Their understanding is
Universal human need,
Body, mind and spirit.
They show their secret suffering.
Would you like to see,
Generation care?

25/03/2021

36. Fulfil Universal Need

We don't want to make money.
It's not our core being,
It's not who we are,
It doesn't satisfy,
It doesn't suit.

We want to meet the needs of everyone on the planet.
That's finite,
That's possible,
That's respectable,
The planet can cope with that.

We are prepared to make sacrifices for this,
To stop the death of the planet,
To stop the deaths of despair.
It's not infinite consumer choice;
The people and the planet can't cope with that.

To fulfil universal need:
A motivation for mankind,
A valid mission,
A wholesome harmony,
A clear and finite hope,
A beautiful dream,
Mercy and care for all.
Generation Care.

14/04/21

37. Doctor Greedy

Your skills are part of you,
And all the good you do,
You don't need money too,
Dr Succeedy.

Is your income in the sky,
Causing poverty nearby?
Are you consuming too much pie?
Doctor Greedy.

You should be there to care,
But they're dying of despair.
So, is that really fair?
Doctor Greedy.

Is your dollar motivation,
Linked with pharma corporation?
Is it damaging the nation?
Doctor Greedy.

Is your diagnostic action,
Financialized extraction
While you're blind to the reaction?
Doctor Greedy.

Do you generate inequity,
Designing billing weaponry
While public life expectancy,

Eludes you as a remedy?
Doctor Greedy.

Is your system too expensive?
Is your billing too offensive?
Is your public apprehensive?
They're becoming hypertensive,
Doctor Greedy.

Could society be freed,
If we each took what we need?
(Down and outs have needs!)
Will Jesus free you from your greed?
Doctor Greedy.

22/04/2021

38. Adopt a Bottom Line That's Fair

Resentment is the penalty,
For capital's inequity.
Can the planet and people survive,
While so many millions strive,
And so many adverts voice,
Endless consumer choice?
Adopt a bottom line that's fair.
Generation Care?

Could the meaning of life be to care?
Value people and planet as rare?
Could motivation all agree,
The tune of hospitality,
Accentuating human need?
(It does exist, that is agreed).
Adopt a bottom line that's fair;
Generation Care?

Human needs are multiple;
Human needs are physical;
Human needs are mental;
Human needs are spiritual;
Human needs are also social;
Fulfilling everyone is crucial;
Agreeing, seeing and freeing well-being.
Adopt a bottom line that's fair;
Generation Care?

We know humanity is ill,
For those whose needs they can't fulfil.
So power's not the bottom line,
Nor the frequent dollar sign.
Our work to keep our own needs small
Is linked to nurture needs for all.
Adopt a bottom line that's fair.
Generation Care?

With the finite reservations,
And the climate proclamations,
If we're hoping to comply,
Which should labour's yield supply?
Finite needs where poor rejoice,
Or infinite consumer choice?
Adopt a bottom line that's fair.
Generation Care?

Will Jesus Christ return next year,
Removing so much pain and fear,
Will he establish life's welfare?
Need fulfilling everywhere?
Granting our eternal prayer;
Adopt a bottom line that's fair.
Generation Care?

02/04/2021

39. A Scene Irenic

Last night
Was a wonderful night,
A blessed night,
A scene irenic,
In a landscape anaesthetic.

Last night,
Reality fixed,
In a deep sleep.
Gentle,
In a deep sleep.
Quiet,
In a deep sleep.
Calm,
In a deep sleep.
Its integrity,
Its constancy
To keep.

Last night,
Unmoving and high,
Crowds of torn clouds,
In a serene sky.
The moon white hot;
The moon quite round;
Radiant gold,
Its halo surround.

Last night,
Chaos died,
Offence did hide,
Violence dried,
And conflict put aside
In restful peace;
My piece.

Last night,
God,
Fixed in His honesty,
Anchored in his constancy,
Called us back,
To the care we lack,
To restful peace;
Our piece.

27/04/21

40. Call Us Out

Jesus,
Call us out.
Out of our silos,
Into your hallows;
Out of our bunkers,
Into your wonders.
From board rooms and management corridors,
Jesus,
Call us out.

Jesus,
Call us out.
Out of our bed,
Introducing the dead,
And teaching us there,
Compassion and care.
Jesus,
Call us out.

Jesus
Call us out.
Out of the garret,
To show us your merit;
Out of the den,
Your achievements inherit;
Out of the hide,
To your disparate spirit;
Out of the shelter,

Embracing together,
Jesus,
Call us out.

Jesus arise,
In front of our eyes.
Christianise,
Liberalise,
Maximise,
Harmonise,
And synchronise,
Dispelling all doubt.
Jesus,
Call us out.

29/04/21

41. My Fractal Brain

It's insane,
My fractal brain;
A cycle chain,
A neural pain,
A looping train
Of thought.

Autonomous thought
That can't be fought;
Spontaneous thought
In which I'm caught;
Dysfunctional thought,
I haven't sought.

The thoughts that reign
Are quite insane,
An impossible strain.
The powerless slain,
Again, and again,
In my brain.

It's insane,
My fractal brain.
These thoughts must cease,
Control increase,
I need release,
Long lasting peace.

Axe neural pathways of desire,
Neuroplastic change acquire,
Service does my brain rewire,
Creative motives to aspire.

It's insane,
My fractal brain.
Eventually it does repair,
With persistent honest prayer.

02/05/21

42. Social Media

You'll never, never, see,
That my human life is free,
And you're not addicting me,
Mr Robot.

Although you never stop,
I very rarely shop,
So you're not addicting me,
Mr Robot.

I'm speaking face to face,
With people of my race,
Not living in your space,
Mr Robot.

My time belongs to me,
Not an advert jamboree,
Or an addict's gallery.
It's a living family,
Mr Robot.

Your money-making vulture,
Is damaging our culture,
Alienating one another,
Mr Robot.

You augment our group beliefs,
Silo culture, you increase,
Now we're fighting in the streets,
Mr Robot.

You've got us on your hook,
Because consumers like to look,
But will it overcook?
Mr Robot

When will you learn to care?
And, can you learn what's fair
When you're not even aware?
Mr Robot.

07/05/21